COOKBOOK OF THE FLAVORS OF THE DIET OF FORAGED ANIMALS

100 SIMPLE AND TASTY GAME MEAT RECIPES

ELLA FISHER

All rights reserved.

Disclaimer

The information contained in this eBook is meant to serve as a comprehensive collection of strategies that the author of this eBook has done research about. Summaries, strategies, tips and tricks are only recommendation by the author, and reading this eBook will not guarantee that one's results will exactly mirror the author's results. The author of the eBook has made all reasonable effort to provide current and accurate information for the readers of the eBook. The author and its associates will not be held liable for any unintentional error or omissions that may be found. The material in the eBook may include information by third parties. Third party materials comprise of opinions expressed by their owners. As such, the author of the eBook does not assume responsibility or liability for any third party material or opinions. Whether because of the progression of the internet, or the unforeseen changes in company policy and editorial submission guidelines, what is stated as fact at the time of this writing may become outdated or inapplicable later.

The eBook is copyright © 2022 with all rights reserved. It is illegal to redistribute, copy, or create derivative work from this eBook whole or in part. No parts of this report may be reproduced or retransmitted in any reproduced or retransmitted in any forms whatsoever without the writing expressed and signed permission from the author.

TABLE OF CONTENTS

TABLE OF CONTENTS..4

INTRODUCTION..8

    EATING GAME...9
    POPULAR GAME MEAT...10

VENISON..13

    1. VENISON STEAKS...14
    2. ELK JERKY..16
    3. VENISON-SPINACH SALAD................................19
    4. GRILLED PUMPKIN AND BEER SAUSAGES........22
    6. INJERA CASSEROLE..28
    5. CURRIED VENISON NUGGETS...........................31
    6. VENISON MEATBALL SOUP................................34
    7. VENISON STEW...37
    8. VENISON JERKY..40
    9. BARBECUED VENISON.......................................42
    10. SMOTHERED VENISON CUBES.......................44
    11. VENISON CHILI..47
    12. TEXAS CHILI..51
    13. VENISON SOUP...53
    14. BUCK AND BOURBON......................................55
    15. VENISON OR MOOSE STEAK...........................58
    16. GAME SAUSAGE...60
    17. VENISON SAUSAGE...63
    18. TANGY VENISON KABOBS..............................65
    19. COMPANY VENISON STEW.............................68
    20. VENISON SALAMI...70
    21. STUFFED HEARTS..72

WILD BOAR 75

22. Wild Boar Cutlets 76
23. Roast Wild Boar 78
24. Wild Boar Stew with Blueberries 81
25. Wild Boar Ragù 84
26. Slow Cooker Wild Boar 87
27. Braised Wild Boar with Citrus-Sage Sauce 90

CHAMOIS 94

28. Sous-vide chamois leg 95
29. Chamois curry 97

PHESANT 101

30. Baked Pheasant with Marinade 102
31. Smothered Pheasant 104
32. Pheasant and Apple Casserole 106
33. Pheasant in Cream 108
34. Barbecued Pheasant 110
35. Pheasant Steaks 113
36. Parmesan Pheasant 115
37. Braised Pheasant with Mushrooms 118
38. Deep Fat-Fried Pheasant 120
39. Pheasant Breasts in Rice 122
40. Pheasant Fondue 124
41. Pheasant Balls 126
42. Pheasant and Rice Soup 128
43. Pheasant Soufflé 131
44. Pheasant Pot Pie 134
45. Pheasant Ala King 137
46. Pheasant Loaf 140
47. Pheasant Croquettes 142
48. Pheasant Patties 145
49. Pheasant Hash 148

DUCK **150**

    50. PEKING DUCK 151
    51. SMOKED WHOLE DUCK 154
    52. BLACK BOTTOM DUCK 157
    53. SPICY ROAST DUCK 159
    54. WILD DUCK IN SOY MARINADE 161
    55. DUCK FILETS 163
    56. TEXAS BARBECUED DUCK 165
    57. DUCK GUMBO 167

DOVES **170**

    58. BRAISED DOVE IN VEGETABLES 171
    59. GRILLED DOVES 174
    60. BRAISED DOVE WITH WILD RICE 176
    61. DOVES WITH RICE IN MARSALA 179
    62. BARBECUED DOVE BREASTS 181

QUAIL **183**

    63. TEXAS QUAIL 'N BACON 184
    64. QUAIL OVER VEGETABLE AND HAM STRIPS 186
    65. STUFFED QUAIL 188
    66. QUAIL ON A BED OF LEEKS 190
    67. QUAIL WITH SOUR CREAM AND BACON 192

RABBIT **194**

    68. CHEESY RABBIT POT PIE 195
    69. GRILLED RABBIT WITH VEGETABLES 198
    70. ONE DISH RABBIT AND SWEET POTATOES 201
    71. RABBIT CREOLE 204
    72. PULLED BARBEQUE RABBIT 207
    73. PULLED RABBIT TACOS 210

GOOSE **213**

    74. GREEN CURRIED SNOW GOOSE 214

75. Snow Goose Fajitas..217
76. Snow Goose in Pesto...220
77. Stir Fried Snow Goose...222
78. Snow Goose Medallions...224
79. Snow Goose T-Bone Steak......................................227
80. Snow Goose Gumbo...229
81. Szechuan Snow Goose..233
82. Snow Goose Stew..236
83. Snow Goose Cutlets..239
84. Seasoned Snow Goose..241
85. Snow Goose Runza...244
86. Snow Goose Pie..247
87. Smoked Hawaiian Snow Goose..............................250
88. Snow Goose Cassoulet..253
89. Snow Goose and Wild Rice Casserole....................256
90. Crumbled and Fried Beaver Tail............................260

BISON..**262**

91. Bison Meatloaf...263
92. Bison Stroganoff..266
93. Bison Dirty Rice..269
94. Ground bison and vegetable stew..........................272
95. Bison Skillet..275
96. Salisbury Steak..278

MARINADES..**283**

97. Hunter Sauce...284
98. Marinade for Game...286
99. Marvelous Marinade...288
100. Sweet-Hot Dip for Venison.................................290

CONCLUSION..**292**

INTRODUCTION

Eating Game

Game meat from wild animals is delicious, low fat and sustainable. Enhanced by the natural flavours of the animals foraged diet, game meat is generally more flavoursome than farmed meat. Cooking game can be simple and tasty, whether you've hunted it yourself or got it from a good butcher or game dealer like the Wild Meat Company.

Many people are put off game food which can be overly fussy – they don't have to be! Use pheasant instead of chicken in a curry or pan fry partridge breasts for a quick weekday supper. Make a delicious rabbit ragu instead of the usual beef or treat yourself to a venison, rather than beef, steak at the weekend.

This book aims to inspire you to cook game more often and show you just how simple and delicious it can be.

Popular Game Meat
- A. **Pheasant**: Probably the most popular and widespread game bird is pheasant. Young birds are delicious when roasted, while older birds can be casseroled, braised or pot roasted. If you're a novice when it comes to cooking game, start with pheasant as it has a sweet, earthy flavour that isn't overpowering.
- B. **Grouse:** Considered by many to be the finest game bird there is. It has dark, rich red meat and an intense taste which holds up well to strong flavours. You can keep it simple and roast with lots of butter at high temperature.
- C. **Duck:** Wild duck including mallard, pigeon and teal are available in autumn and winter but it's mallard that you are most likely to come across. Wild duck has a richness that lends itself to a variety of dishes, with less fat and a stronger flavour than farmed duck.

D. **Goose:** Wild goose has a rich dark meat and gives off a strong fragrance while cooking. Butchers and game dealers are not allowed to sell wild goose so if you want to try one, you'll either have to shoot your own or be given one by someone who has!

E. **Venison:** With lean low fat meat, venison is an increasingly popular alternative to other red meats. Wild venison has an edge over farmed having dark red meat with rich flavour resulting from its varied, natural diet. The different species of deer vary in flavour and texture, with fallow being finer textured than the mighty red, while the tiny muntjac has the mildest flavour.

F. **Rabbit:** Wild rabbit is one of the tastiest and most abundant game meats there is and we should eat more of it! It is very low fat. People liken it to chicken but in fact wild rabbit is stronger flavoured with a darker meat. Young rabbits can be roasted whole and the meat torn off, older ones (the best indicator is size) can be tougher and are better braised or slow cooked in a stew or curry.

VENISON

1. Venison Steaks

Ingredients:

- 3 T. flour
- 1½ t. salt
- ¼ t. marjoram leaves
- 6 venison steaks, cut from the round
- Fat for frying
- 1 small onion, peeled
- 4 medium carrots, peeled
- ½ c. diced celery and tops 1½ c. beef broth

Directions:

a) Mix flour, salt and marjoram; rub over meat. Brown steaks in hot fat in pressure pan. Add vegetables and broth; cover, and cook at 10 lbs. Pressure 20 to 30 minutes, or as manufacturer directs. Cool normally 5 minutes, then place pan under cold water to reduce pressure quickly.

b) Thicken liquid for gravy by rubbing vegetables through sieve, food mill or blender. Serves 6.

2. Elk jerky

Ingredients:
- 2 pounds lean elk
- ½ cup Worcestershire sauce
- ¼ cup blackstrap molasses
- ¼ cup dark soy sauce
- 1 teaspoon finely grated lemon zest
- 1 teaspoon caraway seeds
- 8 cardamom pods, cracked
- 3 garlic cloves, finely minced
- Neutral cooking oil

Directions:

a) Remove as much fat from the meat as you can and freeze the meat for 20 to 30 minutes to make it easier to slice. With a very sharp knife, slice the meat as thinly as you possibly can ¼ to ⅓ inch thick.

b) In a large bowl, whisk together the Worcestershire sauce, molasses, soy sauce, lemon zest, caraway seeds, cardamom, and garlic.

c) Drop the sliced meat into the bowl one piece at a time to ensure that each piece is completely coated in the brine. Allow the meat to sit in the marinade for 90 minutes. Remove the meat and discard the marinade. Now it's time to dry the meat either in the oven or with a food dehydrator.

3. Venison-Spinach Salad

Serves 2

Ingredients:
Vinaigrette:

- 1 cup chopped strawberries
- 2/3 cup extra virgin olive oil
- 1/2 cup distilled white vinegar
- 2 cloves garlic, minced
- 1 1/2 teaspoons poppy seeds
- 1 teaspoon salt
- Fresh ground black pepper to taste

Venison

- 1 venison steak
- Salt and pepper to taste
- 3-4 cups baby spinach leaves
- 1 cup sliced strawberries

- 1/4 cup sliced almonds

Directions:

a) Prepare the grill on medium-high.

b) Season the venison with salt and pepper and grill for about 5 minutes per side or until cooked to desired doneness. Let the venison stand for 10 minutes, then slice.

c) Toss the spinach with strawberries and place on plates. Sprinkle with the almonds and top with the sliced venison.

d) Drizzle the vinaigrette over the salad and serve immediately.

e) **For Vinaigrette:** Combine all the ingredients into a food processor or blender and puree until smooth.

4. Grilled pumpkin and beer sausages

Yield: 1 Serving

Ingredients:
- 1 Bottle ale beer
- 4 ounces Pumpkin; fresh or canned
- 1-ounce Garlic; Diced
- 1-ounce Pure maple syrup
- 2 Links each duck; pierced with a fork
- 2 Links venison; pierced with a fork
- 2 Links chicken sausage; pierced with a fork
- 1 small Red onion; Segmented thin
- 1 tablespoon Butter
- Salt
- Pepper
- 1 Bulb fennel; shaved
- 1 ounce Each saga bleu cheese
- 1 ounce English stilton
- 1-ounce Gorgonzola

Directions:

a) Mix porter, pumpkin, garlic and maple syrup and spurt over sausages.

b) Take out sausages from brine and roast in a 500-degree grill for 10 minutes. Segment and grill up until done.

c) Cook onions in butter over low heat up until soft and translucent. Season with salt and pepper

5. Roast kudu fillet with boerewors stuffing

Yield: 1 servings

Ingredient

- Kudu fillet
- 500 grams Venison
- 200 grams Pork
- 125 grams Lamb's kidney fat
- 1 teaspoon Salt
- 1 tablespoon Crushed roasted coriander seeds
- 50 millilitres Red wine
- 50 millilitres Malt vinegar
- 1 pinch Ground cloves
- 1 pinch Thyme
- 1 pinch Oregano
- 2 Banana shallots; finely diced
- 200 millilitres Pinotage
- 200 millilitres Demi-glace

Directions:

a) Mince venison, pork and fat together, making sure that it is not too fine.
b) Combine all ingredients, mixing well, and put aside.
c) Clean the kudu fillet well and split down the middle. Fold out and pack with the boerewors, fold the meat back over and tie with string. Rub salt and pepper on outside with a little olive oil.
d) To cook place into a hot pan or on to a chargrill, turning frequently, and allow to cook until the boerewors has firmed up. Slice thickly and serve.
e) For the pinotage sauce, sweat off the finely diced shallots and add the red wine (pinotage) a little at a time allowing it to reduce by at least two thirds. Add the demi to the wine slowly until a thick, dark consistency is achieved. Check taste and serve.

6. Injera Casserole

Serves: 2

Ingredients

- 2 pounds venison, cut into bite-sized pieces
- 1 Injera torn into pieces
- ¾ teaspoon salt
- 40 grams (⅓ cup) diced purple onions
- 2 tablespoons olive oil
- 1 tablespoon minced garlic
- ⅓ cup water
- 1 Cup green beans
- 2 tablespoons dry white wine
- 1 tablespoon + 1 teaspoon berbere paste
- 1 tablespoon tomato paste
- 10-15 very soft dates, seeded and halved or cut

Directions

a) In a large skillet, add olive oil and cook venison and onion until the meat is no longer pink; drain. Add the beans and salt.
b) Transfer to a greased 13x9-in. baking dish. Arrange Injera over the top.

c) Combine garlic, water, white wine, berbere paste and tomato paste in a bowl; pour over tortillas. Sprinkle with cheese.
d) Bake, uncovered, at 350° for 25-30 minutes or until heated through.
e) Add the dates and cook for another minute.

5. Curried Venison nuggets

Ingredients

- 1-pound venison, cut into chunks
- 4 tablespoons Thai red curry paste
- 1 large Egg
- oil for frying
- Breading
- 1/2 cup grated parmesan cheese
- 1/2 cup pork panko
- 1/2 teaspoon Homemade Seasoned Salt

Chipotle Ranch Dip

- 1/4 cup mayonnaise
- 1/4 cup Sour Cream
- 1 teaspoon chipotle paste to taste
- 1/2 teaspoon Homemade Ranch Dressing and Dip Mix
- 1/4 medium lime, juiced

Directions

a) For the Chipotle Ranch Dip: Combine all ingredients, mix well
b) Combine Pork Panko, parmesan cheese and seasoned salt.

c) Beat 1 egg and curry paste in 1 bowl and breading mix in another.
d) Dip chunks of steak in egg, then breading. Place on a wax paper lined sheet pan or plate.
e) Freeze breaded raw steak bites for 30 minutes before frying.
f) Heat oil to roughly 325 degrees F and fry steak nuggets until browned, about 2-3 minutes.
g) Transfer to a paper towel lined plate, season with a sprinkle of salt and serve with Chipotle Ranch.

6. Venison meatball soup

Ingredients:

- ½ pounds Lean venison or lamb,
- Ground twice
- ½ cup Cooked rice, ground wheat
- ¼ cup Finely chopped onion
- ¼ cup Finely chopped parsley
- 2 cans Condensed chicken broth
- 2 cans Water
- ⅓ cup Lemon juice
- 2 Eggs
- Salt, pepper

Directions:

a) Combine first four ingredients. Shape into ¾-inch balls. Heat broth and water to the simmering point. Add meatballs; simmer 15 to 20 minutes. In a soup tureen, beat lemon juice and eggs until smooth.

b) Gradually beat in hot broth. Add meatballs last. Season to taste with salt, pepper.

7. Venison Stew

Ingredients:

- 2 lbs. Venison stew meat, cut in 1½ inch cubes
- 3 T. fat
- 4 c. boiling water
- 1 T. lemon juice
- 1 t. Worcestershire sauce
- 1 clove garlic
- 1 large onion, sliced
- 2 bay leaves
- (optional: 2 t. salt or to taste)
- 1 t. sugar
- ½ t. pepper
- ½ t. paprika
- Dash of ground allspice
- 6 carrots, sliced
- 12 small white onions, peeled
- 3 potatoes, peeled and cut in large cubes

Directions:

a) Sauté the meat on all sides in hot fat until brown. Add water and all ingredients except the three vegetables.

Cover, simmer 2 hours stirring occasionally to keep from sticking (or bake in a slow oven - 300-325/F) for 2 hours.

b) Remove bay leaves and garlic. Add carrots, onions, and potatoes. Cover. Continue cooking 30 more minutes or until vegetables are done. Thicken the liquid for gravy. Serves 6-8.

8. Venison Jerky

Ingredients:

- 2 lb. lean venison, trimmed of all fat
- ½c. pickling salt ¼ c. brown sugar
- ½t. black pepper
- ½t. garlic powder

Directions:

a) Cut strips of meat as thin as possible; inch or less by 4-6 inches long. Combine remaining ingredients to make a dry brine. Roll pieces quickly in dry brine solution and place on rack in smoker. The temperature in the smoker should stay between 75 and 95/ for 10-12 hours or until jerky strips snap when bent.

b) Jerky can be cured with no salt or brine mix at all. It can be dried plain, only it will just take longer to be dry enough. The salt brine will allow the jerky to keep longer.

9. Barbecued Venison

Ingredients:

- 1-28 oz. bottle prepared barbecued sauce
- 1 cup ketchup
- 2 T. pickle relish
- 1 cup beef broth or pan juices venison roast
- 1 small onion, chopped
- 2 branches celery, chopped
- 2 lbs. cooked rump roast of venison

Directions:

a) Mix all ingredients except venison in a large saucepan. Cook over low heat about 30 minutes or until sauce is thick.

b) Slice rump roast into the bubbling sauce and simmer until meat is just heated through.

c) Makes 5 servings of 2 hearty sandwiches per person.

10. Smothered Venison Cubes

Ingredients:

- 2 lb. venison stewing meat Flour for dredging
- Fat
- 2 medium onion, cut up
- 2 cloves garlic, cut fine
- 2 t. grated Cheddar cheese
- 2 t. salt
- ½ t. pepper
- 2 c. water
- 5 t. barbecue sauce
- 1 small can mushrooms or ¼ lb. sliced mushrooms (optional)

Directions:

a) Remove any visible fat from meat. Cut meat into 1-inch cubes; dredge in flour, and brown in hot fat.

b) Add onions and garlic; brown lightly. Add cheese salt, pepper, water and barbecue sauce.

c) Cover and simmer about 1 hour and 30 minutes; stir occasionally to prevent sticking. Add mushrooms before thickening gravy.

11. Venison Chili

Ingredients:

- ½ lb. pinto or red beans
- 4 lbs. coarsely chopped venison (neck, flank, plate, brisket, round, hind, shank) 1½ t. cumin seed
- ½c. chopped suet or sowbelly cut in julienne strips
- 6 good-size onions, chopped
- 2-4 cloves garlic, minced
- 1 t. oregano
- 3 T. fresh chili powder
- 1 large can Italian peeled tomatoes
- 1 small can green chilies
- Salt and pepper
- Dash of Tabasco sauce (optional)
- 2 T. instant masa harina or cornmeal

Directions:

a) Wash the beans, cover with fresh cold water, bring to boil, and simmer 2 minutes; let stand, tightly covered, 1 hour. Prepare meat (stewing cuts are best if fat-free) by cutting into 1-inch cubes.

b) Put cumin seeds in a skillet over medium heat and keep them moving until they smoke and turn toast-colored; then spread them on a flat surface and crush with a rolling pin. Now melt the suet or sowbelly in a large skillet; you may substitute enough vegetable oil or other shortening to coat the bottom of the pan, but you'll lose meaty flavor.

c) As soon as the fat is rendered or begins to sizzle add pieces of meat a few at a time and sear, turning cubes to seal all sides.

d) Lower heat and add onions and garlic, stirring occasionally until onions are translucent. Add parched cumin seed, oregano, and the freshest chili powder you can get; stir to coat meat with seasonings, add tomatoes and green chilies, and bring to boiling point, then reduce heat to simmer.

e) Bring the soaking beans to a boil again and allow to bubble almost imperceptibly until they are tender - 30 minutes to an hour, depending upon beans.

f) Meanwhile watch the meat mixture to see that it is not getting too dry, adding water or stock as necessary to maintain a rather fluid consistency. Taste for seasoning, adding salt and pepper if necessary, and a dash of Tabasco as your taste buds decree.

g) After about $1\frac{1}{2}$ hours (time will depend upon quality and toughness of venison cuts) sample the meat; if tender skim off the excess grease - or refrigerate overnight to let the fat coagulate for easy removal. Add masa harina for thickening.

h) Then combine chili with cooked beans, bring back to simmering point, and allow flavors to meld for another 30 minutes.

12. Texas Chili

Ingredients:

- 2 lbs. venison stew meat
- 1 lb. lean pork or javelina, diced or ground
- ½ c. cooking oil
- 2 large onions, chopped
- 3 cloves garlic, minced
- 6 c. beef stock
- 6 T. chili powder 1 t. cumin seed, crushed
- Salt and pepper

Directions:

a) In a Dutch oven, heat the oil and sauté' the onions and garlic for five minutes; then set aside. Brown the meat and pour off the oil.

b) Return the onions and garlic to the oven and add beef stock, chili powder and cumin seeds. Stir and bring to a boil.

c) Reduce heat, cover, and simmer for at least an hour. Add a little salt to taste. Add pepper if needed. Simmer for a few more minutes and serve.

13. Venison Soup

Ingredients:

- 2 or 3 lbs. venison bones with some meat
- 1-16 oz. pkg. Frozen soup vegetables
- 1 T. parsley
- 1 clove garlic, minced
- Salt and pepper
- 1-16 oz. can tomatoes

Directions:

a) Put the bones into a Dutch oven and cover them barely with water. Simmer for two hours. Remove the bones and pull off any remaining meat with a fork. Dice any large chunks. Save three cups of the stock and discard the rest.

b) Add the meat, frozen vegetables, parsley, garlic, salt and pepper. Mash or chop the tomatoes and put them into the pot, along with the juice from the can.

c) Stir, bring to a quick boil. Reduce heat to very low, cover tightly and simmer for an hour. Add a little water if needed.

d) Then add a little more pepper and serve.

14. Buck and Bourbon

Ingredients:
- 2-2½ lbs. venison, cut in 1½" cubes
- 5 T. flour
- 1 t. salt
- ¼ t. pepper
- 1½ T. oil or lard
- 2 medium onions, diced
- ½ c. chopped green pepper
- 2 cloves garlic, diced
- 1 cup tomato sauce, canned or homemade
- ½ t. thyme or crushed rosemary (or both)
- 3 oz. bourbon
- ½ c. water with bouillon cube

Directions:

a) In a skillet (with a lid for later use) brown over slow to medium fire the meat cubes shaken or rolled in flour, salt and pepper. Don't crowd the meat pieces, but brown in the oil or lard and remove as they are ready, then set aside.

b) Sauté the onions, green pepper, and garlic in same skillet until soft.

c) Add browned meat cubes and remaining ingredients, cover and simmer slowly for about 1½ hours.

15. Venison or Moose Steak

Ingredients:

- 4-5 onions
- 3 green peppers
- 18-20 mushrooms
- ¼ lb. butter
- 2 bay leaves
- 3-4 lb. venison or moose steaks, 1½-2" thick Salt and pepper
- 4 garlic cloves, smashed

Directions:

a) Dice onions, green peppers and mushrooms. Take a cast-iron frypan and fry these up in the butter with the bay leaves. Then take the steak and rub salt, pepper and smashed garlic cloves

b) into the meat on both sides. Fry with onions and peppers. Do not overcook, as this will make it tough.

16. Game Sausage

Ingredients:
- 1 small onion, chopped
- 2 cloves garlic, chopped
- 6 oz. pork fatback, cut in chunks
- 1 cup dry sherry
- ½lb. red game flank
- ½lb. venison stew meat ¼ c. chopped parsley 1 t. thyme
- 1 T. kosher salt
- ½t. coarsely ground black pepper
- 1 T. Worcestershire sauce
- 2 t. fennel seed
- 2 t. caraway
- Pinch of saltpeter
- Sausage casings, soaked for 30 minutes in warm
- water

Directions:

a) Sauté the onion and garlic in the fatback slowly until limp and golden. Add the sherry and cook more rapidly 4-5 minutes.

b) Cut the two meats in rough chunks and then put into the food processor or through the medium blade of a grinder along with the onion-garlic mixture and the remaining ingredients.

c) Fry a dab of this mixture and taste to see if it is highly seasoned enough; if not, correct. If you don't have a sausage stuffer, use a plastic bag.

d) Slide a length of the soaked casing up over the funnel. Tie a knot in the far end. Force the stuffing through the funnel. After the casing is about $2\frac{1}{2}$ inches full, twist it and tie it up, then continue until the sausage meat is used up. Tie a knot at the end of the casing.

e) TO COOK: Simmer the sausage in water to cover, lightly salted and peppered. They should be cooked through in 15 minutes.

17. Venison Sausage

Ingredients:

- 10 lb. venison
- 10 lb. pork
- $\frac{1}{4}$ lb. salt
- 4 or 5 garlic cloves, crushed
- 3 T. crushed red peppers
- 8 T. rubbed sage
- 4 lb. sausage casings

Directions:

a) Grind venison and pork together once, add seasonings, mix and grind twice more. Stuff meat into casings, which have been thoroughly washed, or make into patties.

b) When serving, allow about $\frac{1}{2}$ lb. per person. Place in heavy skillet with enough water to cover bottom of pan. Cook covered over medium-low heat, 30 to 45 minutes. Remove cover and brown. Makes about 40 servings. Store in the freezer.

18. Tangy Venison Kabobs

Ingredients:

- 1½ to 2 lb. venison, cut into 1" cubes
- ¾ c. bottled Italian Salad Dressing
- ¼ c. lemon juice
- 1 T. Worcestershire Sauce
- ¼ c. minced green onion
- 2 small green peppers, halved and quartered
- 1 medium onion, cut into wedges
- 8 fresh mushrooms
- 8 cherry tomatoes

Directions:

a) Combine dressing, lemon juice, Worcestershire and onion in glass casserole dish. Add meat, cover and marinate in refrigerator, turning meat occasionally for 4 hours or overnight.

b) On kabob skewer, thread bell pepper, venison, onion, mushroom, repeat starting with bell pepper.

c) Brush with remaining marinade. Place kabobs on cooking grill or charcoal (one layer) and cook approximately 10 minutes, turning occasionally.

d) Top with cherry tomato, turn kabob over, brush with marinade and cook an additional 5 minutes or until desired doneness.

e) Makes 4 servings (2 kabobs each).

19. Company Venison Stew

Ingredients:

- 6 oz. lean bacon
- ¾ c. flour ½ t. flour t. pepper
- 3 lb. 4 oz. venison, cubed
- 1 lb. onion, chopped
- 1 lb. carrots, thickly sliced
- 1 large can ripe olives, pitted
- 3½ c. beef broth
- Red wine
- 1 T. vinegar
- 3 oz. tomato paste
- 1 garlic clove, minced
- ¾ t. thyme, crushed
- 1 Bay leaf
- c. parsley, chopped

Directions:

a) Combine flour, salt and pepper and dredge venison cubes. In a large crock pot layer bacon, venison cubes, and vegetables.

b) Combine beef broth and remaining ingredients. Pour over all and simmer on high 8-12 hours or until fork tender.

20. Venison Salami

Ingredients:

- 2 lb. ground venison
- 1 cup water
- 2 T. Curing salt
- 1 T. Liquid Smoke
- 1 T. garlic powder
- 1 T. onion powder
- 1 t. fresh cracked pepper
- 1 T. fresh pepper corns
- 1 t. cumin
- 1 T. mustard seed
- $\frac{1}{4}$ t. cayenne pepper

Directions:

a) Mix all ingredients together and roll into small rolls about $1\frac{1}{2}$" in diameter.

b) Refrigerate for 24 hours to let flavors develop. Place on sheet pan and bake at 300/ for 30-45 minutes.

21. Stuffed Hearts

Ingredients:

- 2-3 deer hearts, depending on size, or 1 moose heart
- 1 cup fresh bread crumbs
- 1 cup minced ham
- 1 cup finely chopped suet
- 1 egg, lightly beaten
- ¼ c. chopped parsley
- 1 sprig marjoram, chopped, or ¼ t. dried
- 1 sprig rosemary, chopped, or ¼ t. dried
- 1 t. grated lemon peel
- Salt and freshly ground pepper
- 3 strips bacon
- 2 T. flour
- 2 c. boiling water
- 2 t. tomato paste

Directions:

a) Soak the hearts in cold water for 1 hour. Remove the veins and arteries with a sharp knife, then wash out and dry hearts.

b) Prepare the stuffing by mixing the bread crumbs, ham, suet, egg, herbs and lemon peel together. Taste and salt and pepper as desired. Make a 2- 3 -inch slash on one side of each heart and fill with the stuffing. Wrap each stuffed heart with a strip of bacon and secure it with a skewer.

c) Place hearts upright in an earthenware casserole and bake in a 350/ oven for 2-3 hours, until meat is tender. Remove the hearts to a heated platter. To the pan drippings add the flour, stir, and cook a minute or so.

d) Off heat pour in the boiling water and tomato paste, then return to the heat and stir as the sauce thickens. Simmer a few minutes, then serve in a sauce-boat along with the hearts.

WILD BOAR

22. Wild Boar Cutlets

- 2 lb. wild boar cutlets
- 1 cup buttermilk
- 1 t. salt
- 3 juniper berries, crushed
- 1 T. soft butter
- 1 T. flour

Directions:

a) Submerge cutlets for 3 days in buttermilk in refrigerator. Drain and dry, then rub with salt and crushed juniper. Preheat oven to 350/. Cover bottom of roasting pan with $\frac{1}{4}$-inch of boiling water and place meat on rack grazing water. Roast 1 hour, basting occasionally with buttermilk.

b) Meanwhile blend together the butter and flour with your fingertips. When the meat is tender and does not bleed when pierced, stir the butter-flour past into the liquid in the roasting pan. Stir until thick and smooth and adjust seasoning.

23. Roast Wild Boar

SERVES 4
Ingredients:

- Ingredients send grocery list
- 1 onion, roughly chopped
- 4 cloves garlic, minced
- 2 carrots, roughly chopped
- 2 celery stalks, roughly chopped
- 1/2 bulb fennel, roughly chopped
- 1/2 cup olive oil, divided
- salt and pepper to taste
- 1 1/2 pounds wild boar roast
- 6 sprigs fresh thyme
- 3 sprigs fresh rosemary
- 1 tablespoon fresh oregano
- 1/2 cup water

Directions:

a) Heat oven to 375 degrees.
b) Toss the chopped vegetables (onion, 2 garlic cloves, carrots, celery and fennel) in 1/4 cup of olive oil and season with salt and pepper. Lay them in the bottom of a small roasting pan and set aside.
c) Heat a skillet on high heat until very hot.
d) Season the roast with salt and pepper. Add a tablespoon of olive oil to the skillet and sear the roast on all sides.

e) While the meat is searing, take about half of the amount of fresh herbs you have and chop them finely. Place the chopped herbs in a small bowl, and add the remainder of the minced garlic and olive oil; stir to form a loose paste.
f) After the boar has been seared, rub it all over with the paste and set atop the vegetables in the roasting pan.
g) Tie the remaining herbs together with butcher's twine and throw into the roasting pan.
h) Add the water to the pan, then cover the pan and roast for 1/2 hour, or as long as it takes to reach an internal temperature of 155-160 with a meat thermometer.
i) Allow to rest about five minutes before slicing and serving with the roasted vegetables.

24. Wild Boar Stew with Blueberries

Ingredients:

- 1-kilogram wild boar (diced, shoulder or leg)
- 1 1/2 tablespoons vegetable oil
- 1 onion (finely sliced)
- 2 carrots
- 1 Orange (organic)
- 1 clove garlic
- 1 clove
- 1 cinnamon stick
- 4 juniper berries
- 2 pinches nutmeg
- 2 bay leaves
- 2 tablespoons cognac
- red wine (1 liter.)
- 4 tablespoons beef stock
- 2 tablespoons blueberry jam
- 200 grams fresh blueberries
- 2 tablespoons flour (optional)
- chicken broth

Directions:

a) Brown the cubed meat in a pan with the oil, then remove the meat and set aside.
b) In the same pan, sauté the onions (thinly sliced) and carrots.
c) Add the orange zest, crushed garlic, cloves, cinnamon stick and juniper

berries, then season with salt and pepper, sprinkle with nutmeg, and add the bouquet garni.
d) Return the meat to the pot and add the brandy, if desired flambé it.

25. Wild Boar Ragù

Ingredients:

- 1-pound wild boar shoulder or leg, cut into 1- to 2-inch pieces
- 1 rosemary sprig, torn in half
- 4 garlic cloves, peeled
- 2 cups Chianti or other red wine, or as needed
- 3 tablespoons extra-virgin olive oil
- 1 small carrot, finely chopped
- 1 small celery stalk, finely chopped
- 1 small onion, finely chopped
- 1 cup canned tomatoes, with their liquid
- 2 cups vegetable stock or water
- Tagliatelle or other pasta, for serving

Directions:

a) The night before making the ragù place the meat in a bowl with the rosemary, peppercorns, garlic and enough wine to cover. Cover and refrigerate overnight.

b) Discard the rosemary and garlic. Drain the meat in a strainer set over a bowl, reserving the wine. In a Dutch oven over medium-high heat, heat the oil until shimmering, and add the carrot, celery and onion. Sauté until softened, 3 to 5 minutes.

c) Add the meat and cook, stirring frequently, until all the liquid released by the meat has evaporated and the meat is browned, 10 to 15 minutes. Add the reserved wine and cook, stirring frequently, until the mixture is dry, 10 to 15 minutes.
d) Add the tomatoes, breaking them up with a spoon. Add 1 cup water, reduce heat to very low, and cook, partly covered, at a low simmer for 1 hour.
e) Add vegetable stock and continue to simmer, stirring occasionally, until the meat begins to break apart, 1 1/2 to 2 1/2 hours. Remove from heat and, using a whisk or spoon, break the meat into very fine shreds.
f) Serve, if desired, over tagliatelle or other pasta.

26. Slow Cooker Wild Boar

Ingredients:

- 5-6-pound wild boar shoulder roast or a conventional pork shoulder
- olive oil to coat roasts
- 2 tablespoons of Montreal Steak Seasoning or more
- 1 onion with skin on -chopped
- 2 carrots – rough cut
- 1 bunch parsley – chopped
- 6 cloves garlic
- 1 in small can diced tomatoes juice or paste
- $\frac{1}{2}$ cup bourbon
- $\frac{1}{2}$ cup brown sugar

Directions:

a) Cut roast into two manageable pieces
b) rub roast with olive oil and season liberally, set aside
c) Chop the vegetables for your slow cooker
d) Heat a large sauté pan on your stove top and when pan is very hot add a little olive oil and sear both sides of your roast.
e) Place cut veggies and garlic in bottom of your slow cooker.
f) Add the roast, bourbon, brown sugar and diced tomatoes.

g) cover slow cooker and cook on low for approx. 7 hours.
h) The sauce that is in the bottom of the slow cooker should be strained and placed in a small sauce pot, reducing the liquid by half over a medium – high heat.
i) Serve the wild boar in pieces, encouraging your guests to pull it into pieces dipping it the sauce that came from the slow cooker or your favorite sauces.

27. Braised Wild Boar with Citrus-Sage Sauce

Ingredients:

- 4.4 pounds saddle of wild boar (ready to cook)
- 3 bay leaves
- 1 teaspoon ground allspice peppers
- ½ cup game stock (or chicken broth)
- 2 pints unfiltered apple juice
- 7 ounces shallots
- 2 garlic cloves
- salt
- 2 tablespoons clarified butter
- 2 oranges
- 2 small grapefruit
- 4 fresh sage (leaves)

Directions:

a) Rinse boar meat, pat dry and place in a large freezer bag (6 liters).
b) Add bay leaf, allspice, pepper, stock and apple juice. Seal the bag tightly and turn bag to coat meat. Marinate for 8-12 hours (preferably overnight) in the refrigerator.
c) Peel the shallots and garlic. Dice garlic and cut shallots into quarters.
d) Open freezer bag, pour marinade into a large bowl, remove meat and pat dry with paper towels. Score the layer of fat with

a sharp knife in a diamond-shaped pattern and rub the meat on all sides with salt and pepper.

e) Heat the butter in a roasting pan and cook meat over high heat on all sides. Add shallots and garlic and cook until softened.

f) Pour marinade into pan, cover and cook in preheated oven at 180°C (fan 160°C, gas: mark 2-3) (approximately 350°F) for about 2 1/2 hours, turning regularly.

g) Remove lid and raise temperature to 200°C (fan oven 180°C, gas: mark 3) (approximately 400°F). Turn the meat, fat side up, and cook until it forms a nice crust, about 30 minutes more in the oven.

h) Meanwhile, use a sharp knife to cut peel off oranges and grapefruit, so that all bitter white pith is removed. Cut out the fruit between membranes, working over a bowl to collect the juices.

i) Remove meat from pan and cover to keep warm. Remove bay leaves and pour cooking liquid into a pot. Bring to a boil and boil for about 10 minutes more.

j) Rinse sage, shake dry, pluck leaves and chop finely.

k) Add citrus segments and collected citrus juice with the sage to the sauce and cook for about 5 minutes. Season with salt and pepper.
l) Cut meat into slices and serve with the citrus-sage sauce.

CHAMOIS

28. Sous-vide chamois leg

Ingredients

- 500 g Chamois leg, boneless, prepared by the butcher
- 200 ml Red wine, dry
- 200 ml Wild fund
- 6 Date, without stone
- 2 Tablespoons Apple Cider Vinegar
- 2 Tablespoons clarified butter
- 2 Onion, red
- 1 teaspoon Venison Seasoning

Directions:

a) Total time approx. 2 hours 40 minutes
b) Fry the leg of chamois in clarified butter. Allow the leg to cool down a little and then seal it in foil. Cook in a water bath at 68 degrees for about 2 hours.
c) Cut the onions into sticks, chop half of the dates, cut the other half into slices.
d) Slowly sauté the onion in the frying pan of the leg. Add the chopped dates. Deglaze with red wine, wild jus and apple cider vinegar and reduce to half. Add the game spice and the date slices.

29. Chamois curry

Ingredients

- 2 Chamois shoulders, cut into 4cm chunks on the bone
- 1 onion, finely diced
- 1 bunch of spring onions, roughly chopped
- 4 cloves of garlic
- One knob of ginger
- 2-3 scotch bonnet peppers
- A bunch of thyme
- 2 teaspoons coriander seeds
- 1 teaspoon cumin seeds
- 1 teaspoon fenugreek seeds
- $\frac{1}{2}$ teaspoons mustard seeds
- $\frac{1}{2}$ teaspoons fennel seeds
- 4 cloves
- $\frac{1}{4}$ nutmeg
- $\frac{1}{2}$ teaspoons turmeric
- 20 pimento seeds
- 2 teaspoons cooking oil
- 5 1/2 cups of water or chicken stock
- 2 medium size waxy potatoes, diced.

Directions:

a) Put the onion, spring onion, garlic, ginger, scotch bonnet peppers and thyme in a blender to make a paste. Marinate the meat in the paste for at least two hours, preferably overnight.

b) Grind all the dry spices.

c) Heat 3 Tablespoons oil in a cast iron pot and brown the meat. Season with salt and pepper. Add the ground spices and cover with water.

d) Leave to simmer for 2-2 $\frac{1}{2}$ hours. Add the potato and add a little more water. Leave to simmer till the potatoes are tender. Check the seasoning and add more salt and pepper if needed.

e) Put the rice in a sift, and rinse till the water runs clear.

f) Take a medium sized, heavy bottomed casserole. Add a little oil and sweat the onions till they are soft and translucent. Add the all spice, chili, thyme and salt.

Add the rice and ad the coconut milk and the water. Bring to the boil, cover with baking parchment and a tight-fitting lid.

g) Turn the heat right down and simmer till all the water has evaporated. 10-12 minutes.

h) Let the rice rest for 2-3 minutes with the lid on.

PHESANT

30. Baked Pheasant with Marinade

Ingredients
- 1 dressed pheasant

Marinade:

- 1 cup cooking oil
- 2 Tablespoons minced onion
- 1 teaspoons salt
- l teaspoons black pepper
- 1 small clove garlic, minced
- 1 Tablespoons wine vinegar
- 1 Tablespoons Worcestershire sauce
- 1 teaspoons sugar
- 1 teaspoons tabasco sauce
- 1 teaspoon paprika

Directions

a) Blend marinade thoroughly. Brush pheasant with marinade, tie legs down. Place in baking dish and roast for one hour in a 350°F. oven.

b) Baste every 15 minutes and turn bird once if it doesn't stay upright on its back.

31. Smothered Pheasant

Ingredients
- 1 dressed pheasant, cut into serving pieces
- 3 Tablespoons fat
- 1 cup seasoned flour plus I Tablespoons dry skim milk
- 1 cup light cream

Directions

a) Roll pheasant pieces in seasoned flour and sauté in fat until well browned.
b) Transfer to 2-3-quart casserole. Add cream, cover.
c) Bake in 350° F oven for 1 hour, or simmer 30 to 45 minutes on top of stove.

32. Pheasant and Apple Casserole

Ingredients
- 1 dressed pheasant, cut into serving pieces
- 4 Tablespoons butter or margarine
- 1 teaspoons salt
- 1 teaspoons thyme
- I teaspoons black pepper
- 2 large apples, peeled
- 1 cup apple cider
- 2 Tablespoons wine vinegar
- seasoned flour

Dredge pheasant pieces in seasoned flour.

Brown in butter or margarine over medium heat. Transfer meat to a deep casserole. Sprinkle salt, thyme and pepper over the meat and add sliced apples. Pour cider and vinegar over all. Cover and bake 4 hours at 350°F.

33. Pheasant in Cream

Ingredients
- 1 dressed pheasant, cut into serving pieces
- 1/3 cup butter
- 1 teaspoons salt
- 1 teaspoons thyme
- 1 teaspoon black pepper
- 1 cup flour
- 1 teaspoons onion juice or 1 Tablespoons minced onion
- 1 cup heavy cream

Directions

a) Dredge pheasant pieces in seasoned flour.
b) Brown well in butter. Add onion and cream.
c) Cover and simmer until tender, 30 to 45 minutes.

34. Barbecued Pheasant

Ingredients

- 1 dressed pheasant, cut into serving pieces
- 1 egg, beaten
- 1 teaspoons salt
- 1 teaspoons pepper
- 1 cup bread crumbs
- 3 Tablespoons cooking oil

Barbecue sauce

- 1 Tablespoons vinegar
- 2 c. tomato sauce
- 1 cup diced celery
- 2 Tablespoons diced onion
- 1 Tablespoons brown sugar
- 1 teaspoons thyme
- 1 ts1 Tablespoons vinegar
- 2 c. tomato sauce
- 1 cup diced celery
- 2 Tablespoons diced onion
- 1 Tablespoons brown sugar
- 1 teaspoons thyme
- 1 teaspoons salt
- 1 teaspoons salt

Directions

a) Add salt and pepper to the beaten egg.
b) Roll pheasant pieces in the egg mixture then into crumbs.
c) Brown in the oil over medium heat.
d) Mix the barbecue sauce ingredients and brush over the Pheasant.

35. Pheasant Steaks

Ingredients

- 1 young pheasant, breast and thighs only
- 1 cup flour
- 1 teaspoons salt
- 1 teaspoons pepper
- 1/16 teaspoons oregano
- 1/ 16 teaspoons basil
- 1 cup butter

Directions

a) Pound steaks to even thickness. Mix salt, pepper, oregano and basil with flour.
b) Brown steaks slowly in butter or other shortening (340°-360°F.). Turn when golden brown. To test doneness, cut a gash in center of steak, with a sharp knife.
c) Steaks should still be juicy, without evidence of pink color. Cooking time will be about 3-5 minutes.

36. Parmesan Pheasant

Ingredients
- 1 pheasant, cut in pieces
- 1 teaspoons monosodium glutamate
- 1 cup flour
- 1 teaspoons salt
- 1 teaspoons pepper
- 2 Tablespoons grated Parmesan cheese
- 1 teaspoon paprika
- 1 cup butter
- 1 cup stock

Directions

a) Mix seasonings with flour. Roll pheasant pieces in mixture. If possible, place coated pieces on a rack to dry about 1 hour.

b) Brown slowly in butter in skillet (340° - 360°F.). Allow 15 minutes on each side. When golden brown, add stock or hot water in which bouillon cube has been dissolved.

c) Cover. Simmer about 20 minutes or until tender.
d) Uncover and cook about 10 minutes longer to crisp.

37. Braised Pheasant with Mushrooms

Ingredients
- 1 pheasant, cut in pieces
- 1 cup pancake mix
- 1 cup butter
- 1 cup mushrooms
- 3 Tablespoons chopped on ion
- 1 cup stock
- 1 Tablespoons lemon juice
- 1 teaspoons salt
- 1 teaspoon black pepper

Directions:

a) Dredge cut up pieces of pheasant in pancake mix.
b) Brown pieces in butter until golden brown (approximately 10 minutes).
c) Remove pheasant pieces.
d) In the butter remaining in skillet, sauté mushrooms and chopped onion until golden brown (approximately I 0 minutes).
e) Return meat to skillet, add stock, lemon juice and seasonings. Cover and simmer 1 hour or until tender.

38. Deep Fat-Fried Pheasant

Ingredients
- 1 young pheasant, cut in pieces
- 1 cup coating mixture
- Milk or buttermilk
- Cooking fat

Directions:

a) Cut meat from each side of keel or breastbone with a sharp knife, making 2 breast pieces. Marinate pheasant pieces in milk or buttermilk 1 to 2 hours in the refrigerator, or dip in milk.

b) Dredge pieces in desired coating. Dry on rack approximately one-half hour.

c) Transfer a few pieces at a time to deep fat basket and lower into heated fat (350° -360° F.). Use 2 inches or more of heated fat.

d) Remove pieces when golden brown (3-5 minutes).

e) Serve immediately.

39. Pheasant Breasts in Rice

(4 servings)

Ingredients
- 4 pheasant breasts
- 1 can mushroom soup
- 1 envelope dry onion soup mix
- 1 cup milk
- 1 cup rice
- 1 cup mushroom bits

Directions:

a) Combine soups and milk. Pour half of the mixture into an oblong baking dish (approx. 7x 11 inches).
b) Stir in rice and mushroom bits. Arrange pheasant breasts on the rice mixture, press down and pour the remainder of the soup mix over the breasts.
c) Cover with foil and bake 1 hour and 15 minutes in a 3 50°F oven. Uncover the last 15 minutes to brown.

40. Pheasant Fondue

Ingredients
- 1 dressed pheasant cut into bite-sized pieces
- 2 c. vegetable oil

Directions:

a) Heat oil in electric fondue pot to 425°F.
b) Shake excess moisture from pheasant pieces, spear on fondue fork and place in hot oil. Fondue about one minute or till golden brown. Remove from fork, salt if desired, ready to eat.

41. Pheasant Balls

(3-4 servings)

Ingredients
- 1 cup ground raw pheasant
- 1 egg, slightly beaten
- 2 Tablespoons minced onion
- 1 teaspoons salt
- 1 teaspoon paprika
- 1 teaspoons pepper
- 2 Tablespoons fat or oil
- 1 cup bread crumbs and/or cornflake crumbs

Directions:

a) Mix pheasant, egg, onion and spices together.
b) Make about seven meatballs 1-inch in diameter (rounded tablespoon). Roll in crumbs.
c) Brown in fat until brown and meat is done. Medium heat about 15 minutes.

42. Pheasant and Rice Soup

(4 servings)

Ingredients
- 1 dressed pheasant, cut in pieces
- water to cover

Soup:
- 1 qt. broth
- 1 carrot diced (1/3 to! c.)
- 2 Tablespoons diced onion
- t c. diced celery
- 1 cup diced cooked pheasant
- 2 Tablespoons rice
- I teaspoons celery salt
- ! teaspoons salt or more to taste
- t teaspoons pepper

Directions:

a) **For the pheasant:** Boil 30 to 40 minutes until meat is tender and will come off the bones easily. Cool. Remove meat from bones and strain the broth.

b) **For the soup:** Combine all ingredients and simmer 15 minutes. This can be made in advance and reheated to serve. Serve with crisp cracker's.

43. Pheasant Soufflé

(4 servings)

Ingredients

- 1 cup cubed cooked pheasant
- 2 eggs, separated
- 1 cup cooked white rice
- ! c. fresh bread crumbs
- ! c. diced celery
- 1 cup milk
- 1 teaspoons salt
- 1 teaspoon black pepper
- 1 teaspoons thyme

Directions:

a) Beat egg yolks and add all ingredients but egg whites. Beat egg whites until stiff and fold into mixture.

b) Pour into heavily-greased flat baking dish or an 8 x 8-inch square dish.

c) Bake at 350°F for about 30 minutes, or until a knife inserted in center comes out clean.

d) Cut into squares and serve with mushroom sauce.

44. Pheasant Pot Pie

(2-3 servings)

Ingredients
- 1 cup cubed cooked pheasant
- 1 cup diced onion
- 1 cup thinly sliced carrot
- 1 cup frozen peas (! pkg.)
- 1 bay leaf
- 1 chicken bouillon cube
- 1 cup water
- 1 cup medium white sauce
- Rich biscuit topping

Directions:

a) Optional seasonings: chili powder, cumin, Worcestershire sauce, savory, thyme, mace, marjoram or a combination of any of these spices.

b) Boil vegetables, bay leaf and bouillon cube in water until tender (about 10 minutes). Drain and save liquid for sauce.

c) Combine liquid and enough milk to make 2 cups liquid.

d) Make sauce with 3 Tablespoons butter, 3 Tablespoons flour and 1 teaspoons salt.

e) Combine pheasant, vegetables and white sauce with additional seasonings optional. Put into 3 qt. casserole and top with baking powder biscuits. Bake at 450°F for 15 minutes.

45. Pheasant Ala King

2 servings

Ingredients
- 1 cup cubed cooked pheasant
- 1 Tablespoons butter or margarine
- 1 Tablespoons flour
- ! c. broth or chicken bouillon
- 1 cup heavy cream
- 1 teaspoons salt
- dash of pepper
- 1 Tablespoons minced onion
- 1 egg yolk, beaten
- 2 slices of toast or English Muffins

Directions:

a) Melt margarine with onion in sauce pan, stir in flour.

b) Add broth and cream, heat slowly without boiling. Pour this mixture into beaten egg yolk. Add salt, pepper and pheasant.

c) Heat only till hot. Serve on buttered toast points or English muffins.

46. Pheasant Loaf

(3-4 servings)

Ingredients
- 1 cup finely diced cooked pheasant
- 2 Tablespoons minced onion
- 2 Tablespoons minced green pepper
- 1 teaspoons salt
- 1 teaspoons nutmeg
- 1 teaspoons pepper
- 1 cup dry bread crumbs
- 2 eggs beaten
- 1 cup milk
- 1 Tablespoons Worcestershire sauce

Directions:

a) Combine first seven ingredients. Beat eggs

b) and mix in milk and Worcestershire sauce. Add liquid to dry mixture. Blend thoroughly. Put into a buttered loaf pan and bake 45 minutes in a 350°F oven. If a longer loaf pan is used, reduce baking time accordingly.

47. Pheasant Croquettes

(Makes 10-12 croquettes)

Ingredients
- 1 cup chopped cooked pheasant
- 4 Tablespoons butter or margarine
- 4 Tablespoons flour
- 1 cup milk
- 1 teaspoons salt
- 1 teaspoons marjoram
- 1 teaspoons curry powder
- 1 egg, beaten
- 2 Tablespoons flour
- 1 cup bread crumbs and/or corn flake crumbs

Directions:

a) Make a sauce of flour, butter and milk, add meat and seasonings. Chill thoroughly. Beat egg.

b) Shape croquette mixture, roll in flour, egg and then crumbs, being sure all areas are coated with egg before crumbing.

c) Deep fat fry at 375°F about 5 minutes or until golden brown, drain on absorbent paper, serve hot.

48. Pheasant Patties

7-8 patties (4 servings)

Ingredients
- 2 c. diced cooked pheasant (do not grind)
- 1 cup toasted bread crumbs
- 4 Tablespoons butter or margarine (divided)
- 1 cup minced onion
- 2 Tablespoons minced green pepper
- 1 egg, slightly beaten
- 1 cup milk
- 1 teaspoons Worcestershire sauce
- 1 teaspoons salt
- 1 teaspoons thyme
- 1 teaspoon black pepper
- 1 cup corn flake crumbs

Directions:

a) Melt 2 Tablespoons butter or margarine in fry pan over medium heat, cook onion and green pepper until golden brown. Blend pheasant, crumbs and seasonings. Spoon vegetables out of fat and add with the egg, milk and Worcestershire sauce. Mix thoroughly and let set a few minutes to blend flavors.

b) Spoon out rounded tablespoon of mixture into crumbs, coat with crumbs and with the aid of a spatula transfer to medium hot fry pan.

c) Fry until golden brown, using 2 Tablespoons of butter or margarine as needed, turn once (1 0-15 minutes overall cooking time).

d) Do not overcook as they become dry. This mixture is hard to handle but good enough to warrant patience in making the patties. Mushroom sauce may be served with the patties for a change.

49. Pheasant Hash

(3-4 servings)

Ingredients

- 1 cup cooked pheasant meat
- 1 potato
- 2 teaspoons minced green pepper
- 2 teaspoons minced onion
- 1 Tablespoons pimento
- 1 teaspoons salt
- 1 teaspoons pepper
- 2 Tablespoons fat

Directions:

a) Put pheasant and potato through food

b) grinder with medium to coarse blade. · Add pepper, onion and pimento and seasonings. Brown

c) in fat for 15 minutes, stirring occasionally.

DUCK

50. Peking duck

Servings: 4-6

Ingredients

- 4½ lb.s. whole duck
- 2 Tablespoons liquid honey
- 1 Tablespoons Szechuan peppercorns
- 1 Tablespoons sea salt
- 1 Tablespoons Chinese five-spice powder
- 1 Tablespoons baking soda
- 6 spring onions, roughly chopped
- 3½ ounces fresh ginger, roughly chopped

To serve

- Ppancakes
- 1 bunch of spring onions
- ½ a large cucumber, cut into thin slivers
- Hoisin sauce

Directions

a) Massage the honey all over the duck.

b) In a pestle and mortar, crush the Szechuan peppercorns and sea salt to a coarse powder. Stir in the Chinese five-spice powder and baking powder.

c) Spread the mixture evenly over the duck, massaging it into the honeyed skin.

d) Stuff half of the spring onions and ginger into the cavity.

e) Roast for 25–40 minutes in a hot wood oven, rotating the tin halfway through to ensure even crisping.

f) Halfway through cooking, flip the duck over to crisp up the underside as well.

51. Smoked Whole Duck

Ingredients:

- 5 pounds whole duck (trimmed of any excess fat)
- 1 small onion (quartered)
- 1 apple (wedged)
- 1 orange (quartered)
- 1 Tablespoons freshly chopped parsley
- 1 Tablespoons freshly chopped sage
- ½ teaspoons onion powder
- 2 teaspoons smoked paprika
- 1 teaspoons dried Italian seasoning
- 1 Tablespoons dried Greek seasoning
- 1 teaspoons pepper or to taste
- 1 teaspoons sea salt or to taste

Directions:

a) To make rub, combine the onion powder, pepper, salt, Italian seasoning, Greek seasoning and paprika in a mixing bowl.

b) Insert the orange, onion, and apple to the duck cavity. Stuff the duck with freshly chopped parsley and sage.

c) Season all sides of the duck generously with rub mixture.

d) Place the duck on the grill grate.

e) Roast for 2 to 21/2 hours, or until the duck skin is brown and the internal Smoke Temperature of the thigh reaches 160°F.

52. Black Bottom Duck

Ingredients:

- 3 wild or domestic ducks
- 4 T. lemon juice
- ½ c. melted butter

Baste

- 1 cup liquid from roast pan
- ½ t. flour
- 2 t. brown sugar
- 1 T. wine vinegar
- Juice of ½ orange
- 1 t. grated orange rind

Directions:

a) Tighten the liquid with the flour. Caramelize sugar over low flame, add vinegar, orange juice, and rind. Add to the thickened liquid and pour over the ducks.

b) Clean, singe, and rub ducks inside and out with lemon juice. Roast at 425/ 10 minutes for each pound of duck. Baste with butter. Boned ducks are wonderful. When finished, baste it.

53. Spicy Roast Duck

Ingredients
- 1 wild duck
- 2 T. flour
- ½ t. salt t. pepper
- 1 T. whole allspice, cracked
- 1 bay leaf, crumbled

Directions:

a) Rub duck inside and out with mixture of flour, salt, pepper and allspice. Sprinkle bay leaf pieces over top. Place on rack in roaster (arranging several ducks close together helps prevent drying). Bake, covered, in slow oven (325/) 2½ to 3 hours, or until tender.

b) It's a good idea to wrap each duck in foil the last hour of roasting.

54. Wild Duck in Soy Marinade

Ingredients
- 2 wild ducks, quartered
- 1-13½ oz. can pineapple tidbits
- ½c. soy sauce
- 1t. ground ginger
- ¼c. shortening or bacon drippings
- 1-3 oz. can mushrooms, drained

Directions:

a) Marinate ducks overnight in mixture of pineapple, soy sauce and ginger. Wipe meat; brown in fat.

b) Place in shallow casserole; pour on marinade and mushrooms. Bake, covered in moderate oven (350/) 1½ hours or until tender (add water, if necessary).

55. Duck Filets

Ingredients

- 1 wild duck
- Instant meat tenderizer
- 2 slices bacon
- 2 T. salad oil

Directions:

a) With sharp knife, remove skin from duck. Cut meat from breast in 2 filets. Use meat tenderizer as directed on package. Wrap each filet loosely with bacon slice; fasten with toothpicks.

b) Cook filets in how oil over moderate heat until browned and tender, about 15 minutes per side. Serve on hot platter with ribbons of cooked bacon.

56. Texas Barbecued Duck

Ingredients
- 2 wild ducks
- 2 T. salad oil
- Barbecue Sauce

Directions:

a) Rub ducks with oil; brown under broiler. Brush ducks with half the Sauce; place 1 tablespoon sauce in each cavity. Wrap each bird closely in heavy foil; bake in shallow pan in slow oven (325/) 1 hour, or until tender. Remove foil last 15 minutes, and spoon over remainder of sauce.

b) To Grill Outdoors: Proceed as above, browning over hot coals and finishing over slow coals.

c) **For the Barbecue Sauce:** Sauté 2 tablespoons chopped onion in $\frac{1}{4}$ cup butter. Add $\frac{1}{2}$ cup ketchup, $\frac{1}{2}$ cup lemon juice, $\frac{1}{4}$ teaspoon paprika, $\frac{1}{2}$ teaspoon salt, $\frac{1}{4}$ teaspoon pepper, $\frac{1}{4}$ teaspoon ground red pepper, 2 tablespoons Worcestershire sauce. Simmer 15 minutes.

57. Duck Gumbo

Ingredients

Stock:
- 3 large or 4 small ducks
- 1-gallon water
- 1 onion, quartered
- 2 ribs celery
- 2 carrots 2 bay leaves 3 t. salt
- 1 t. pepper

Gumbo:
- ¾ c. flour
- ¾ c. oil
- 2 garlic cloves, minced
- 1 cup finely chopped onions
- ½ c. finely chopped celery
- 1 c. finely chopped green peppers
- 1 lb. okra cut in ¼" pieces
- 2 T. bacon grease
- 1 lb. raw, peeled shrimp
- 1 pt. oysters and liquor
- ¼ c. chopped parsley
- 2 c. cooked rice

Directions:

a) Skin ducks; boil in water with onion, celery, bay leaves, salt and pepper for approximately 1 hour or until duck meat is tender. Strain; skim all grease and reserve 3 quarters of stock. If needed, add chicken or beef bouillon to make 3 quarts' stock. Remove meat from carcass and bit-size pieces; return to stock. The stock may be made the day before making gumbo.

b) **For Gumbo:** In a large Dutch oven, make a dark brown roux with flour and oil. Add garlic, onions, celery, and green pepper; sauté' okra in bacon grease until all ropiness is gone, about 20 minutes; drain. In a soup pot warm stock and slowly stir in the roux and vegetable mixture. Add okra; simmer covered $1\frac{1}{2}$ hours. Add shrimp, oysters and their liquor, and cook an additional 10 minutes. Stir in parsley and remove from fire. Correct seasoning and serve over hot, fluffy rice. Serves 12.

DOVES

58. Braised Dove in Vegetables

Ingredients

- 6 doves
- 3 T. butter
- 4 shallots or 6 scallions, roughly sliced
- 1 carrot, roughly sliced
- 1 rib celery with leaves roughly sliced
- ½ green pepper, seeded and roughly sliced
- 2 bay leaves
- 1 t. marjoram (or thyme, tarragon or rosemary)
- ½c. boiling liquid, half chicken broth, half white wine ¼ c. sour cream at room temperature

Directions:

a) Sauté the doves in butter until lightly browned in the casserole you intend to use. Set birds aside. In processor or blender reduce the 4 sliced vegetables to a fine mince, but not quite to a puree. Drain, then sauté the minced vegetables in the casserole. Add herbs, the boiling liquid and the birds.

b) Cover and bake at 350/ for 15- 25 minutes. Remove doves. Stir the sour cream into the vegetables and serve as sauce. If it is not thin enough, add sweet cream.

59. Grilled Doves

Ingredients
- ¼ c. oil
- 2 cloves garlic, or shallots, minced
- 1 t. dried rosemary, crumbled
- Salt and pepper
- 6 doves, split down back and flattened

Directions:

a) Mix the oil, garlic or shallots, rosemary, salt and pepper and brush over both sides of the birds.

b) Grill or broil 4-5 inches from heat 7-8 minutes to the side, basting several times with the oil mixture.

60. Braised Dove with Wild Rice

Ingredients
- 1 cup wild rice, washed
- 10 dive breasts
- juice of ½ lemon
- salt and pepper
- 3 T. butter
- 4 shallots or scallions, minced
- 1 rib celery, chopped
- ½ lb. mushrooms
- ½ t. tarragon
- ½ c. dry vermouth or white wine
- 1½ c. chicken broth

Directions:

a) Wash the wild rice until water runs clear. Drain. Skin the dove breasts, rub with lemon juice, and salt and pepper them. In the butter, sauté the shallots or scallions, celery, and mushrooms lightly.

b) Place rice on bottom of casserole, lay in the dove breasts, and add the rest of the ingredients.

c) Cover and bake in a 325/ oven for 1½-1¾ hours.

61. Doves with rice in Marsala

Ingredients
- 1 cup uncooked rice
- 3 T. butter
- 4 doves
- Lemon juice
- Salt and pepper
- ½ t. rosemary, crumbled
- 8 small white onions
- ½ lb. mushrooms
- 1c. chicken broth
- 1c. Madeira

Directions:

a) Sauté the rice in the butter, allowing it to brown but not to burn. Place in the bottom of a casserole. Rub the doves inside and out with lemon juice, then with salt, pepper and rosemary. Place doves on the rice and surround with the onions and mushrooms.

b) Pour broth and Madeira over the doves, cover, and simmer in a 350/ oven for 30-40 minutes.

62. Barbecued Dove Breasts

Ingredients
- 12 dove breasts - young birds
- ½ bottle (18 oz.) barbecue sauce with onion bits
- 1 cup firmly packed brown sugar
- ¼ c. red wine
- ½ t. Worcestershire sauce
- 12 slices of bacon Toothpicks

Directions:

a) Wrap bacon around breast and secure with toothpick. Place on hot gas grill or over one-layer charcoal and brush with sauce.

b) Grill for 10 minutes. Turn, brush with sauce and grill an additional 5 minutes or until done.

QUAIL

63. Texas Quail 'N Bacon

Ingredients
- 10 dove or quail breasts
- 5 medium potatoes, pared and cut in half lengthwise
- 5 slices bacon
- $\frac{1}{2}$ c. bread crumbs
- $\frac{1}{4}$ c. grated Parmesan cheese
- $\frac{1}{4}$ c. wheat germ (optional)
- 1 t. salt Pepper to taste
- $\frac{1}{4}$ stick margarine, melted
- 1 large browning bag

Directions:

a) Cut bacon slices in half. Wrap each dove or quail breast with $\frac{1}{2}$ slice bacon.

b) Combine bread crumbs, Parmesan cheese, wheat germ and salt. Dip potatoes in melted margarine and then in above mixture. Place flat side down in a large browning bag.

c) Roll dove breasts in mixture and place on top of potatoes. Pepper to taste. Bake at 350/ for 1 hour. Serves four to six.

64. Quail Over Vegetable and Ham Strips

Ingredients
- 4 T. vegetable oil
- 1 t. minced fresh ginger
- 3 quail, split
- Salt and pepper
- 3-4 T. chicken broth
- 1 medium zucchini, cut in thin strips
- 1 carrot, scraped and cut in thin strips
- 4 whole scallions, cut in thin strips
- 2 large broccoli stalks, peeled and cut in thin strips
- 2 oz. country ham or prosciutto, cut in thin strips

Directions:

a) In a large skillet or wok heat 2 tablespoons of the oil with the ginger.

b) Brown the quail on all sides. Salt and pepper them. Add a little broth, cover, and steam-braise slowly for 15 minutes.

c) Remove the quail with their juices and keep warm. Serves 2-3.

65. Stuffed Quail

Ingredients
- 1 cup cracker crumbs
- 2 strips bacon, sautéed crisp and crumbled
- 2 T. chopped celery
- 1 cup chicken broth (bouillon broth will do)
- 1 strip bacon for each quail
- 6-8 quail
- Butter
- ½ c. white wine or vermouth

Directions:

a) Preheat oven to 350/. Mix crumbs, crumbled bacon, and celery with ½ cup chicken broth for stuffing. Wrap 1 slice bacon around each quail and hold in place with toothpicks.

b) Place in buttered, ovenproof casserole. Add wine and roast uncovered for 30 minutes. Add liquid from remaining ½ cup broth if more liquid is needed.

66. Quail on a Bed of Leeks

Ingredients
- 8 quail
- 4 T. butter
- 1 T. vegetable oil
- 6-8 leeks, about 2 c., cut into 1" slices
- Salt and freshly ground pepper
- 1 cup heavy cream
- 2 T. chopped parsley

Directions:

a) In a large skillet or a wok sauté the quail in 1 T. butter and the oil, browning quickly on all sides. Remove. Sauté the leeks in the same pan in the remaining butter.

b) Add just a little water to them - no more than 2 tablespoons - cover, and cook slowly for about 10 minutes until the leeks have begun to soften and have absorbed the liquid.

c) Place the quail on top of the leeks, salt and pepper them, then add the cream all around. Cover and cook slowly for 20 minutes. Sprinkle parsley on top when serving. Serves 4.

67. Quail with Sour Cream and Bacon

Ingredients
- 16 quail breast
- 16 slices regular bacon
- 1 cup sour cream
- 1-10¾ oz. can condensed cream of mushroom soup
- 1 cup sliced mushrooms

Directions:

a) Season quail with salt and pepper as desired. Wrap quail with bacon. Combine sour cream and soup with mushrooms.

b) Spoon over birds. Bake, uncovered, at 275/ for 3 hours. Serves 8. Serve over rice.

RABBIT

68. Cheesy Rabbit Pot Pie

Ingredients
- 1 8 oz. package of cream cheese, cubed small
- ½ cup chicken broth
- 3 cups chopped cooked rabbit
- 16 oz. frozen mixed vegetables, thawed
- ½ teaspoons garlic salt
- 1 egg
- ½ cup milk
- 1 cup all-purpose baking mix
- Preferred spices

Directions:

a) Pre-heat oven to 400°F.

b) Cook cream cheese and broth in large saucepan on low heat until cream cheese is completely

c) melted and mixture is well blended, stirring frequently with whisk.

d) Stir in rabbit, vegetables, garlic salt, and other preferred spices; spoon into 9-inch pie plate.

e) Beat egg, milk, and baking mix in medium bowl with whisk until well blended. Stir in baking mix

f) until moistened, then spoon the mixture over the rabbit meat.

g) Place pie plate on baking sheet.

h) Bake 25-30 minutes or until golden brown.

69. Grilled Rabbit with Vegetables

Ingredients
- 4 young rabbit legs (1 lb.)
- ¼ cup vinaigrette dressing, divided
- 1 zucchini and squash, cut into chunks
- 1 red pepper, cut into chunks
- 1 cup cut-up fresh asparagus spears
- 1 small red onion, cut into chunks
- Preferred spices (to taste)
- ¼ cup pineapple chunks (optional)

Directions:

a) Heat grill to medium-high heat.

b) Brush rabbit legs with 2 Tablespoons of dressing, then let stand for 10 minutes.

c) Meanwhile, poke holes in bottom of disposable aluminum foil pan.

d) Toss vegetables with remaining dressing.

e) Place in prepared pan.

f) Sprinkle preferred spices over ingredients

g) Place rabbit legs and a pan of vegetables on grill grate.

h) Grill 20 minutes or until rabbit is done (165°F) and vegetables are crisp-tender, turning rabbit over after 10 minutes and stirring vegetables occasionally.

70. One Dish Rabbit and Sweet Potatoes

Ingredients

- ½ cup Italian dressing
- 3 Tablespoons brown sugar
- 1 Tablespoons chopped fresh thyme
- 1½ lb. sweet potatoes (about 3), cut into 3/4-inch-wide wedges
- 1 young rabbit (3 lb.), cut into 8 pieces

Directions:

a) Heat oven to 375°F.

b) Mix dressing, sugar, and thyme in large bowl.

c) Add potatoes; toss to coat.

d) Transfer potatoes to 15x10x1-inch pan, reserving dressing

e) mixture in bowl.

f) Add young rabbit to reserved dressing mixture; toss to coat.

g) Place in pan with potatoes.

h) Bake for 1 hour or until potatoes are tender and rabbit is done (165°F).

i) Transfer rabbit and potatoes to platter.

j) Strain drippings from pan; pour strained sauce over rabbit.

71. Rabbit Creole

Ingredients
- 1 large, young or adult rabbit, quartered
- 1 can chicken broth or bouillon cube mixed with water
- or other liquid beverage
- 1 can tomato sauce or soup
- 1 medium onion, chopped or sliced
- $\frac{1}{2}$ Tablespoons minced or $\frac{1}{2}$ teaspoons powdered garlic
- 2 teaspoons pepper sauce or spicy peppers
- Salt, pepper, cilantro, and other spices of choice

Directions:
a) Mix broth and seasonings in stew or crock pot,
b) or roasting pan.
c) Add rabbit meat.

d) Slow cook until done.

e) Tip: Ideal to serve over rice and beans.

72. Pulled Barbeque Rabbit

Ingredients
- ½ cup chicken broth
- 1 older rabbit
- ½ cup beer or wine, if desired
- ½ Tablespoons garlic or ½ teaspoons garlic powder, if desired
- ¼ cup chopped onion, if desired
- BBQ spices and sauce
- 2 bay leaves

Directions:

a) Slow cook all ingredients in liquid with seasonings of choice in a crock pot or roasting pan until

b) done.

c) After it is cooked all the way through, extract rabbit, and allow the meat to rest (drain and cool).

d) Pull rabbit meat from bones once it is cool enough to handle.

e) Return pulled meat to crock pot or pan, add barbeque sauce to taste.

f) Reheat meat with BBQ sauce.

73. Pulled Rabbit Tacos

Ingredients
- ½ cup chicken broth
- 1 older rabbit
- ½ cup beer or tequila, if desired
- ½ Tablespoons garlic or ½ teaspoons garlic powder, if desired
- ¼ cup chopped onion, if desired
- All your preferred Mexican type spices/seasonings; or, you can use a commercial taco mix packet
- 2 bay leaves
- Taco shells
- Condiments: shredded lettuce, chopped tomatoes, cheese, salsa, sour cream, and jalapeño

Directions:

a) Slow cook rabbit in liquid with above ingredients and seasonings of choice in a crock pot or roasting pan until done.

b) Cool after it is cooked all the way. Remove rabbit meat and let it rest (drain and cool).

c) Pull meat off bones, place back into crock pot or pan, and add seasonings to taste.

d) Reheat pulled rabbit meat.

e) Serve once it is thoroughly reheated.

f) Move to serving dish.

g) Load taco shells and garnish as desired.

GOOSE

74. Green Curried Snow Goose

Ingredients
- 2 SNOW GEESE, cut in 1" cubes
- 24 ounces coconut milk, canned
- 2 tablespoons oil
- 2 tablespoons fish sauce
- 1 teaspoon salt
- 4 tablespoons coriander leaves, fresh chopped
- 3 tablespoons curry paste, green
- 2 green chiles, fresh chopped
- 1 tablespoon grated lemon rind

Directions:

a) Simmer half the coconut milk and oil over medium-high heat for 4-5 minutes, or until it begins to thicken.

b) Add curry paste and simmer for 5 minutes while stirring constantly.

c) Add goose meat and cook over medium-high heat for about 15 minutes.

d) Add the remaining half of coconut milk, lemon rind, salt and fish sauce.

e) Stir until the mixture begins to boil.

f) Reduce heat, remove cover and simmer for 35 minutes.

g) Add chopped chilies and herbs. Simmer 5 minutes.

75. Snow Goose Fajitas

Ingredients
- 1-pound SNOW GOOSE meat, cut into thin strips
- 1 green pepper
- 1 red pepper
- 1 yellow pepper
- 1 red onion
- 4 ounces beer or apple juice
- 2 tablespoons oil
- 2 tablespoons chili powder
- 1/2 lime, squeezed
- 1/4 teaspoon cayenne pepper
- salt and pepper to taste
- flour tortillas
- salsa
- sour cream

Directions:
a) Slice all vegetables into strips.

b) Heat oil in cast iron frying pan until smoking hot. Add goose meat and spices.

c) Stir fry quickly until meat is medium rare, then add vegetables and fry, still on high heat until vegetables are tender-crisp (about 3-5 minutes).

d) Add beer or apple juice and squeeze of lime, continue to stir until well mixed.

e) Serve from pan to tortilla and garnish with salsa and sour cream to taste.

76. Snow Goose in Pesto

Ingredients

- 3 pounds SNOW GOOSE meat, sliced
- 3 cups white wine
- 3/4 cup pesto sauce
- 1 teaspoon fennel seeds, crushed
- 1 teaspoon caraway seeds
- 1 teaspoon coriander, ground
- 1/2 teaspoon sugar

Directions:

a) Marinate goose meat in white wine overnight in fridge.

b) Drain meat.

c) Brown meat in electric skillet. Add fennel, sugar, coriander, caraway and pesto.

d) Simmer for 1 hour.

77. Stir Fried Snow Goose

Ingredients
- SNOW GOOSE meat, sliced 1/2" thick
- 1 cup teriyaki sauce
- 1 cup white wine
- 5 teaspoons five-spice powder
- 3 cups Chinese vegetables, sliced

Directions:

a) To make marinade, mix teriyaki sauce, white wine and five spice powder.

b) Marinate meat for 2-4 hours (the longer the better). Drain.

c) Stir fry in hot wok or black skillet in sesame oil. Add vegetables and fry until vegetables are tender-crisp.

78. Snow Goose Medallions

Ingredients
- 1 SNOW GOOSE breast
- 1/3 cup cognac
- 1/3 cup white wine
- 1/3 cup cream
- 2 tablespoons clarified butter
- flour for dredging
- salt and pepper to taste

Directions:

a) Mix flour with salt and pepper to taste. Lightly flour the sliced goose meat.

b) Quickly sauté in the clarified butter over medium-high heat. After having sautéed the meat, set aside in separate dish. (Do not overcook.)

c) Deglaze the pan with the cognac first, then the wine. Once the alcohol is burned off, slowly stir in the cream. Cook until well blended and thickened.

d) Pour over the sautéed goose meat and serve.

79. Snow Goose T-Bone Steak

Ingredients

- 2 SNOW GOOSE breasts, sliced 1/2' thick

- 1/2 cup Caesar salad dressing

Directions:

a) Marinate meat overnight in salad dressing.

b) Heat up a Teflon pan on high.

c) Put breasts in pan and sear the meat surface.

d) Reduce heat and cook to medium rare.

80. Snow Goose Gumbo

Ingredients

- 4 whole SNOW GEESE, boned and skinned
- 1 whole chicken, cut into cubes
- 4 quarts' water
- 28 ounces stewed tomatoes, canned
- 1 pound smoked sausage, chopped
- 1-pound okra, frozen, sliced
- 2 cups white onions, chopped
- 2 cups green bell pepper, chopped
- 1 cup oil
- 3/4 cup flour
- 3 tablespoons creole seasoning
- 1 tablespoon Tabasco sauce
- 2 teaspoons black pepper
- 1 teaspoon Sassafras leaves, finely ground

Directions:

a) In a large pot, cover whole chicken with water (about 4 quarts). Boil until the meat falls off the bone (about 1/2 hour).

b) Remove bones and skin, and leave chicken meat in broth and save.

c) In a large iron skillet, combine oil and flour, cook at medium high and stir continually until it browns. This is what Cajuns call a roux and forms the basis of many of their foods.

d) Once the roux is made, add onions, green pepper, goose meat and smoked sausage. Cook it all for approximately 10 minutes. Then add all to the large pot of chicken broth.

e) Season with creole seasoning, black pepper, cayenne pepper and tabasco.

f) Bring to a boil while stirring, then let simmer for a couple of hours.

g) Add stewed tomatoes and okra. Boil for 15 minutes. Add a little more water if necessary (I don't like it too thick) and simmer until ready to eat. After it has simmered a bit, taste the liquid to see if more spice is needed. If you do add more spice, simmer a little bit more to blend the flavours.

h) About 5 minutes before eating, add the sasafras (gumbo file) and stir well.

i) Leftover gumbo freezes well. Take a frozen batch to the duck camp if you do not have time to spend cooking. It gets better as it ages (spicier too)!

81. Szechuan Snow Goose

Ingredients

- 2 SNOW GEESE, skinned and boned, 1/4-inch-thick strips
- 2 eggs
- 4 tablespoons corn starch
- 2 teaspoons salt
- 4 cloves garlic, chopped
- 1 large onion, chopped
- 1/4 cup chicken stock
- 3 tablespoons soy sauce
- 2 tablespoons fresh ginger root, minced
- 2 tablespoons ketchup
- 2 tablespoons hoisin sauce
- 2 tablespoons sherry or rice wine
- 1 tablespoon hot peppers, diced
- 1 tablespoon sugar
- 1 tablespoon red wine vinegar

- 1 teaspoon chili peppers, dried and crushed

Directions:

a) Blend egg, salt and cornstarch into thin batter. Coat meat with mixture.

b) Cook in deep fryer. Remove, drain and set aside.

c) Heat oil in a large skillet, add garlic, onion, ginger, hot and chili peppers and sauté over high heat for 2-3 minutes or until onion just starts to brown.

d) Add chicken stock, soy sauce, ketchup, hoisin sauce, sherry or rice wine, red wine vinegar and sugar and stir over medium-high heat until sauce thickens.

e) Add the cooked goose and cook over low heat for an additional 5 minutes.

82. Snow Goose Stew

Ingredients

- 2 pounds SNOW GOOSE meat, cubed
- 2 packages fresh linguini or fettuccine
- 1-pound shrimp, large, uncooked, peeled
- 2 large Italian sausages, spicy, sliced
- 1 cup mushrooms, chopped
- 4 shallots, chopped
- 1 can cream of mushroom soup, condensed
- 1 red pepper, chopped
- 3/4 cup grated parmesan cheese
- 1 teaspoon savory

Directions:

a) Sauté together goose meat and sausages for 5 minutes in a skillet.

b) Drain.

c) Put mushroom soup into saucepan. Add goose and sausage. Stir. Add mushrooms, shallots, red pepper and savory. Stir. Simmer on low heat.

d) Add fluid (water/wine) if required. If fresh mushrooms are used, there will be enough fluid generated. Simmer for at least 30 minutes to conclude cooking and blending of flavours.

e) Add shrimp, cook without boiling, for an additional 3-5 minutes. 15 minutes before serving, prepare pasta.

f) Place pasta in a large bowl. Cover with stew and sprinkle with parmesan cheese.

83. Snow Goose Cutlets

Ingredients
- 1 Snow Goose breast, halved
- flour
- salt and pepper to taste
- 1 egg
- 3/4 cups milk
- 1 cup crackers, finely ground

Directions:

a) Slice breasts horizontally, so that three flat, oval fillets are made per half a breast.

b) Coat breast by rolling in flour, spiced with salt and pepper. Beat egg and milk together.

c) Dip coated fillet in egg and milk mixture. Then roll fillet in soda crackers. Fry in hot oil until golden brown and meat has been cooled to medium rare (about 3 minutes per side).

84. Seasoned Snow Goose

Ingredients

- 4 SNOW GOOSE breasts, filleted
- 8 slices bacon
- 1 1/2 sticks butter, sliced
- 1 bay leaf, crushed
- 1 tablespoon poultry seasoning
- 1 teaspoon parsley
- 1 teaspoon salt
- 1 dash black pepper
- 1 dash red chili peppers
- 1 dash cinnamon

Directions:

a) Preheat oven to 350°F.

b) Rinse fillets. Wrap bacon around fillets and arrange in baking dish lined with a large piece of aluminum foil.

c) Add butter slices, sprinkle with seasonings and seal foil tightly at top.

d) Bake for 1 1/2 hours.

85. Snow Goose Runza

Ingredients
- 1-pound SNOW GOOSE meat, coarsely ground
- bread dough, enough for one loaf
- 6 slices Canadian bacon, finely chopped
- 5 cups cabbage, chopped
- 1 cup onions, chopped
- 1 cup cheddar cheese, grated
- 2 tablespoons caraway seed
- 1/2 bay leaf, ground
- salt and pepper to taste
- water

Directions:

a) Preheat oven to 350°F.

b) Spread bread dough out to 1/4 inch of raised dough. Cut into 6" by 6" squares.

c) Lightly sauté the goose meat with the bacon. Add salt and pepper to taste.

d) Transfer from skillet to mixing bowl. Sauté cabbage and onions in same skillet. Transfer to same mixing bowl.

e) Add caraway, bay leaf and cheese.

f) Mix thoroughly and spread the mixture onto each of the dough squares. Coat the edge of dough with water or egg whites and pinch shut.

g) Bake in oven for 1 1/2 hours.

h) This freezes well, and can be microwaved to thaw and eat.

86. Snow Goose Pie

Ingredients

- legs and breasts from 2 SNOW GEESE
- 4 beef bouillon cubes
- 2 cups potatoes, diced
- 1 cup carrots, diced
- 1 cup cold water
- 1/2 cup onions, chopped
- 1/4 cup flour
- 1 garlic clove
- 2 tablespoons seasoned salt
- 1 teaspoon Worcestershire sauce
- 1 10" pie shell, uncooked

Directions:

a) Place the first 6 ingredients in a large Dutch oven and cover with water.

b) Simmer until the meat falls off the leg bones, about 3 to 4 hours.

c) Let cool, remove meat from bones. Discard any meat that is still tough.

d) Chop up the breasts if they have not already fallen apart.

e) Return the meat to the broth in the Dutch oven and add the vegetables.

f) Cook until vegetables are tender, about 30 minutes. Taste to check the seasoning and add a little salt or more seasoning to taste.

g) Blend the flour into the cold water, shaking it in a jar or using a hand blender. Stir into the pie filling; simmer and stir for about 2 minutes.

h) Pour into uncooked pie shell. Cover with top crust, cut slits to allow the steam to escape and bake at 425°F for 10 minutes.

87. Smoked Hawaiian Snow Goose

Ingredients
- 4 SNOW GOOSE breast fillets
- 14 ounces crushed pineapple, canned
- 2 slices bacon
- 3/4 cup honey mustard sauce
- 1/2 cup honey mustard sauce
- 3 tablespoons liquid smoke flavoring
- juice from 1 lemon
- 1/2 teaspoon garlic salt or powder
- pepper to taste

Directions:

a) Mix together olive oil, mustard sauce, liquid smoke flavouring, lemon juice, pepper and garlic spice into a shallow baking pan. Add snow goose breasts and marinate for 18-36 hours.

b) Preheat oven to 325°F.

c) Cook in same pan for 45 minutes with a 3-inch slice of bacon on top of each breast.

d) Add pineapple and cook for another 40 minutes.

88. Snow Goose Cassoulet

Ingredients
- 1-pound SNOW GOOSE meat, cooked and chopped
- 1 pound dried great northern beans
- 1-pound pork sausage, mild
- 1 1/2 cups white wine
- 1 cup onion, chopped
- 1/2 cup dry bread crumbs
- 1/2 cup dry bread crumbs
- 1/2 cup fresh parsley, chopped
- 1/4 cup butter
- 2 sprigs fresh parsley
- 2 cloves garlic
- 1 bay leaf
- 1 sprig fresh thyme or marjoram
- 2 teaspoons salt
- 1 teaspoon black pepper

Directions:

a) Soak the beans overnight in water to cover.

b) Next day, simmer with bay leaf, parsley sprigs, thyme or marjoram sprig, salt, black pepper and one clove of garlic until almost tender.

c) Mince the remaining clove of garlic, and sauté with crumbled sausage and chopped onion until sausage is brown.

d) Arrange a layer of the cooked beans in the bottom of a large casserole dish.

e) Add a layer of goose meat, then more beans and then sausage.

f) Continue layering this way almost to the top of the dish. Now mix the wine and tomato puree, and pour over the casserole. Top with dried bread crumbs mixed with the parsley and butter. Bake in a 350°F until the beans are tender.

89. Snow Goose and Wild Rice Casserole

Ingredients

- 2 cups SNOW GOOSE meat, cubed
- 2 cups water
- 1 1/2 cups evaporated milk
- 1 cup fresh mushrooms, sliced
- 1 cup water chestnuts, canned, drained and sliced
- 1/2 cup wild rice, uncooked
- 1/2 cup sliced almonds
- 1/3 cup water
- 1/4 cup margarine
- 1/4 cup pimiento, drained and sliced
- 3 tablespoons flour
- 2 teaspoons chicken bouillon granules
- 1/2 teaspoon water chestnuts, canned drained, and sliced
- 1/2 teaspoon pimiento

Directions:

a) In saucepan, combine 2 cups water, rice and salt.

b) Heat to boiling, stirring once.

c) Cover and simmer until rice is just tender (30-45 minutes).

d) Drain and set aside.

e) Heat oven to 350°F. Grease 1 1/2-quart casserole dish.

f) Melt butter, add mushrooms. Cook and stir until just tender.

g) Stir in flour, bouillon granules and 1/2 teaspoons salt.

h) Blend in milk and 1/3 cup water.

i) Cook, stirring constantly until thickened and bubbly, about 5 minutes.

j) Remove from heat, stir in goose, water chestnuts, rice and pimiento.

k) Pour into casserole and sprinkle with almonds.

l) Cover and bake for 30 minutes. Remove cover and continue baking another

m) 15-30 minutes, until casserole is hot and bubbly.

90. Crumbled and Fried Beaver Tail

Ingredients
- 1 beaver tail
- 1 cup water
- 1 cup vinegar
- 1 egg, beaten
- bread crumbs
- butter, oil of fat for frying

Directions:

a) Skin the tail, wash it well, then cover it in a pot with water and vinegar. Simmer about $1\frac{1}{2}$ hours or until tender.

b) Drain the meat, which will resemble pork, and cut it into slices as one would for London broil.

c) Dip the slices in beaten egg and roll in bread crumbs. Fry until brown.

BISON

91. Bison Meatloaf

Ingredients

- 1-pound ground bison
- ¼ cup breadcrumbs
- ½ cup beef broth
- 1 egg (beaten)
- ¼ cup grated onion
- ¼ cup shredded Parmesan
- 1 tablespoon tomato paste
- 2 teaspoons Worcestershire sauce
- ¾ teaspoon table salt
- ¼ teaspoon paprika
- ¼ teaspoon black pepper
- ⅛ rounded teaspoon ground sage

Glaze

- ⅓ cup ketchup
- 2 tablespoons balsamic vinegar
- 1 tablespoon brown sugar

Directions:

a) Preheat oven to 350 degrees.

b) Gently crumble bison into a large bowl and add all remaining meatloaf ingredients. Work together to fully incorporate.

c) Mix together glaze ingredients in a separate dish.

d) Paint two tablespoons of glaze on the bottom of a bread pan, or baking pan, and set meatloaf mixture on top of it. Form meatloaf into a loaf 2-3" thick. Then paint the remaining glaze on top of the meatloaf.

e) Place meatloaf in the oven and bake for 40 minutes, or until the internal temperature reaches 160 degrees.

f) Let cool slightly and serve.

92. Bison Stroganoff

Ingredients

- 1 lb. ground bison may substitute lean ground beef
- 2 cans cream of mushroom soup (about 10.5 oz. each)
- 8 ounces' fresh mushrooms sliced
- ¼ cup sour cream
- ½ Tablespoons Worcestershire sauce
- 1 yellow onion diced
- ½ teaspoons onion powder
- ½ teaspoons garlic powder
- ½ teaspoons paprika
- salt and pepper to taste
- For serving
- ½ lb. egg noodles cooked and drained

Directions:

a) Begin by bringing a pot of water to a boil. Add your egg noodles and cook according to the directions on their package. Drain and set aside.

b) Next, brown your ground bison (until no pink remains) with the garlic, mushrooms and the onions. Drain off any fat.

c) Add in the canned mushroom soups, Worcestershire sauce, and sour cream.

d) Sprinkle in the onion powder, paprika, and onion. Stir well then simmer for about 15 minutes.

e) Serve over egg noodles.

93. Bison Dirty Rice

Ingredients

- 1 stalk organic celery, chopped
- 1 small onion, chopped
- 1 green bell pepper, chopped
- 1 Tablespoons olive oil
- salt and freshly ground pepper
- 1-pound ground bison
- 1 Tablespoons Cajun seasoning
- 2 cups Basmati rice (uncooked)
- 4 cups beef broth
- 1 teaspoons GF Worcestershire sauce
- 1 bay leaf
- GF hot sauce

Directions:

a) Add the chopped celery, onion, green bell pepper and EVOO to a 3.5 quart Dutch oven or saucepan. Add a pinch of salt and pepper. Cook over medium heat for about 5 minutes, stirring occasionally.

b) Add the ground bison and Cajun seasoning to the veg mixture. Cook the meat thoroughly, about 5-7 minutes.

c) Remove the pot from the heat and add the uncooked rice. Stir the rice into the mixture so that it is well incorporated. Add the beef broth, bay leaf and Worcestershire sauce. Return the Dutch oven to the stove.

d) Bring to a boil while stirring occasionally, then cover and reduce the heat to low. Cook until done, about 18 minutes.

e) Remove the bay leaf. Taste test for salt and serve with your favorite gluten-free hot sauce.

94. Ground bison and vegetable stew

Servings: 5-6

Ingredients

- 1 lb. ground bison
- 1-2 Tablespoons avocado oil
- 3 large carrots (2 cups), chopped
- 3 celery stalks (1 cup), sliced
- 2 large white sweet potatoes (2 cups), chopped
- 1/2 teaspoons salt
- 2 teaspoons turmeric
- 3 cups chicken broth
- 1 1/2 cups butternut squash, pureed
- 3 cups kale, chopped
- Fresh parsley, topping (optional)

Directions

a) Heat a large pan over medium heat and add the ground bison, breaking into pieces. Once the meat has finished cooking, remove from the pan and set to the side.

b) Heat the avocado oil in a large stock pot on medium heat. Once hot, add the chopped carrots and celery. Sauté for about 8 minutes.

c) Add the white sweet potatoes, salt and turmeric and combine ingredients. Continue cooking the ingredients over medium heat, stirring periodically, for another 10 minutes or until the vegetables have softened a bit.

d) Add in the broth, pureed butternut squash, kale, and bison. Stir all ingredients together and set to low-medium heat, letting the stew simmer for roughly 30 minutes.

e) Once the stew is ready, serve warm and top with fresh parsley if desired.

95. Bison Skillet

Ingredients

- 1 lb. ground bison
- 3 Tablespoons minced garlic
- 1 small onion, diced
- 1 cup fresh minced herbs (we like chives, parsley and oregano)
- 2 cups asparagus, cut into bite size pieces
- 2 cups broccoli, cut in small florets
- ¼ cup avocado oil
- 6 cups mixed greens, split between two plates
- Salt and pepper to taste

Directions

a) Pulse fresh herbs in a food processor until minced. Add half of herbs to a bowl, add bison, garlic and half onion and salt and pepper and mix thoroughly. Form into meatballs.

b) Heat avocado oil in skillet over medium high heat. Add meatballs, remainder of the minced herbs, onion, garlic, asparagus, broccoli and any other vegetables and cook until tender turning the meatballs often to brown on all sides.

c) Divide the salad greens between two plates. Place vegetables and meatballs on the top and serve.

96. Salisbury Steak

Ingredients

- 1-pound Ground Meat: beef, bison, chicken or turkey
- 1 small Yellow Onion grated or finely chopped
- ½ teaspoon chopped Garlic
- 1 teaspoons dried Parsley
- 1 teaspoon Garlic powder
- ¼ teaspoon Kosher Salt
- ¼ teaspoon Black pepper
- ¼ cup Breadcrumbs panko, regular, cracker crumbs; regular or gluten-free
- 1 Egg
- 1 cup All-Purpose Flour (regular or gluten-free measure-for-measure blend)
- ¼ cup peanut Oil or Safflower Oil high smoke point oil
- 2 cups sliced mushrooms
- 1 large Yellow Onion sliced

For the gravy:

- 2 tablespoons Butter or ghee or dairy free butter
- 2 tablespoons All-Purpose Flour (regular or gluten-free measure-for-measure blend)
- 2 cups Stock
- Salt and pepper to taste

Directions

a) In a large mixing bowl, combine ground meat, grated onion, chopped garlic, parsley, garlic powder, breadcrumbs, egg, salt and pepper.

b) Form the mixture into oblong patties (about $\frac{3}{4}$ inch thick) and set aside on a plate. They also can be made smaller into 6 total patties.

c) Add the flour to a shallow bowl and season with salt and pepper.

d) Place a large skillet over medium to medium-high heat on the stove burner and add the oil. TIP: when the surface of the oil is rippling, it's hot and ready.

e) Lightly coat the Salisbury steaks in the flour, then carefully lower them into the hot oil using a spatula.

f) Cook the steaks for 4-5 minutes per side, until browned and crispy, and cooked through the middle. Internal temperatures: beef and bison 160 degrees F. Chicken and turkey 165 degrees F.

g) Remove the cooked steaks from the skillet, then place them on a plate and cover with foil to keep warm.

h) In the same skillet, add the onions and mushrooms. Cook until the onions have softened and started to caramelize, and the mushrooms are softened, stirring often.

i) Remove the cooked onions and mushrooms, and spoon them over the Salisbury steaks.

For the gravy:

j) In the same cooking skillet, melt the butter.

k) Whisk in the flour and cook for a minute or until a paste forms and starts to bubble.

l) Stir in the stock and whisk until thickened and warmed throughout.

m) Season with salt and pepper to taste.

n) Pour over the chicken steaks or into a gravy boat before serving.

o) Serve and enjoy!

MARINADES

97. Hunter Sauce

Ingredients

- ½ c. red currant jelly
- ¼ c. catsup
- ¼ c. port or other sweet red wine
- ½ t. Worcestershire

Directions

a) About 10 minutes before serving: In small saucepan over low heat, cook all ingredients, stirring constantly, until smooth and jelly is melted.

b) Serve with any game or wild birds. Makes 1 cup sauce, enough for 8 servings.

98. Marinade for Game

Ingredients

- 2 c. dry red wine
- 2 T. salad oil
- 2 t. salt
- 1 t. coarsely ground pepper
- ¼ t. thyme leaves
- 2 medium onions, thinly sliced
- 1 garlic clove

Directions

a) In saucepot or Dutch oven, mix all ingredients; add venison or other game; cover and refrigerate overnight.

99. Marvelous Marinade

Ingredients

- A good marinade for wild game or beef:
- 1 cup salad oil
- Lemon juice or 4 T. wine
- ½ t. garlic powder
- ½ t. dry mustard
- ½ t. pepper Worcestershire
- 4 T. sauce
- 2 T. catsup
- Dash of Tabasco

Directions

a) Mix all ingredients in jar; shake.
b) Pour over meat and marinate for 24 hours. Broil in oven or over charcoal.

100. Sweet-Hot Dip for Venison

Ingredients

- Salt and pepper
- 1 T. chopped smoked Cajun ham
- 1 T. each: red and green peppercorns
- 2 T. Cognac
- 1 cup whipping cream

Directions

a) Mix

CONCLUSION

When people talk about eating meat, the images that typically come to mind are beef, turkey, chicken, pork or lamb. However, there is a category of meats from non-domesticated animals—game meats—that also can be found in markets and restaurants near you. Although they represent only a small portion of the market, their popularity is growing.

You have wild game - now, how do you cook it? This cookbook will equip you with the best and easiest game meat dishes!

www.ingramcontent.com/pod-product-compliance
Lightning Source LLC
Chambersburg PA
CBHW051704160426
43209CB00004B/1020